# i KNOW HiM

Written and Illustrated by
## Matt Smeltzer

Graphic Design by
## Nancy Letts

I Know Him

Avid Readers Publishing Group

http://www.avidreaderspg.com

ISBN-13: 978-1-61286-336-8

Printed in the United States

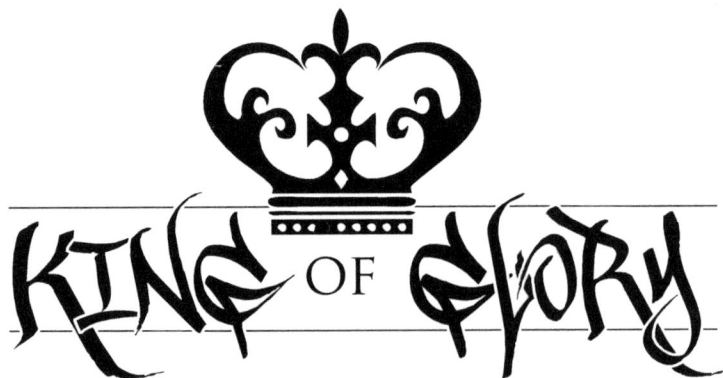

# DEDiCATIONS

I dedicate this book to my children, Rayna, Judah, and Ezekiel.

And it's my prayer, that each of you will always remember that you're deeply loved by Jesus Christ.

- Matt Smeltzer


This book is dedicated to my family, who I love very much.

And my cherished friends who have helped me strengthen my walk with Christ.

- Nancy Letts

A lion, a sheep, and a dove
were visiting near a **tree.**

The lion said,
  "I know the Creator, He's a lot like **me,**
    He's strong, regal, and has **integrity.**"

*Psalm 18:2*

The sheep baa'd and said,
"No, He's more like **me.**
He's gentle, forgiving,
and **comforting.**"

*2 Corinthians 1:3-5*

From up in the tree, the dove cried out,
"No...no, He's more like **me.**
He's truthful, peaceful, and
wants everyone to be **free.**"

*Philippians 4:7*

Then the shepherd appeared
  from behind the **tree**.
He said, "I know Him,
  and He's not like just one of you.
    He's more like all **three**.
His Holy Word shows that He's a **Trinity**."

# TRINITY VERSES

God was manifest in the flesh, justified in the Spirit.
1 Timothy 3:16


Go ye therefore, and teach all nations, baptizing them in the name
of the Father, and of the Son, and of the Holy Ghost.
Matthew 28:19


He is the image of the invisible God, the firstborn of all creation.
For by Him all things were created, both in the heavens and on
earth, visible and invisible, whether thrones or dominions or rulers
or authorities—all things have been created through Him and for
Him. He is before all things, and in Him all things hold together.
Colossians 1:15-17


For there are three that bear record in heaven, the Father,
the Word, and the Holy Ghost: and these three are one.
1 John 5:7

# ABOUT THE
# WRITER AND iLLUSTRATOR

Matt Smeltzer is married to Jolene Smeltzer and is the father of three beautiful children.

He's also a pastor, living in Guatemala with his family as full-time missionaries.

To follow their ministry, please visit kingofglorychurch.wordpress.com/

# ABOUT THE
# GRAPHiC DESiGNER

An avid runner, Nancy Letts is happily married to Kevin Letts. They have an abundance of cats in their home.

Nancy works full-time as a Senior Designer and does calligraphy on the side.

Visit her webpage at lettsgetcreative.com

# Also read...

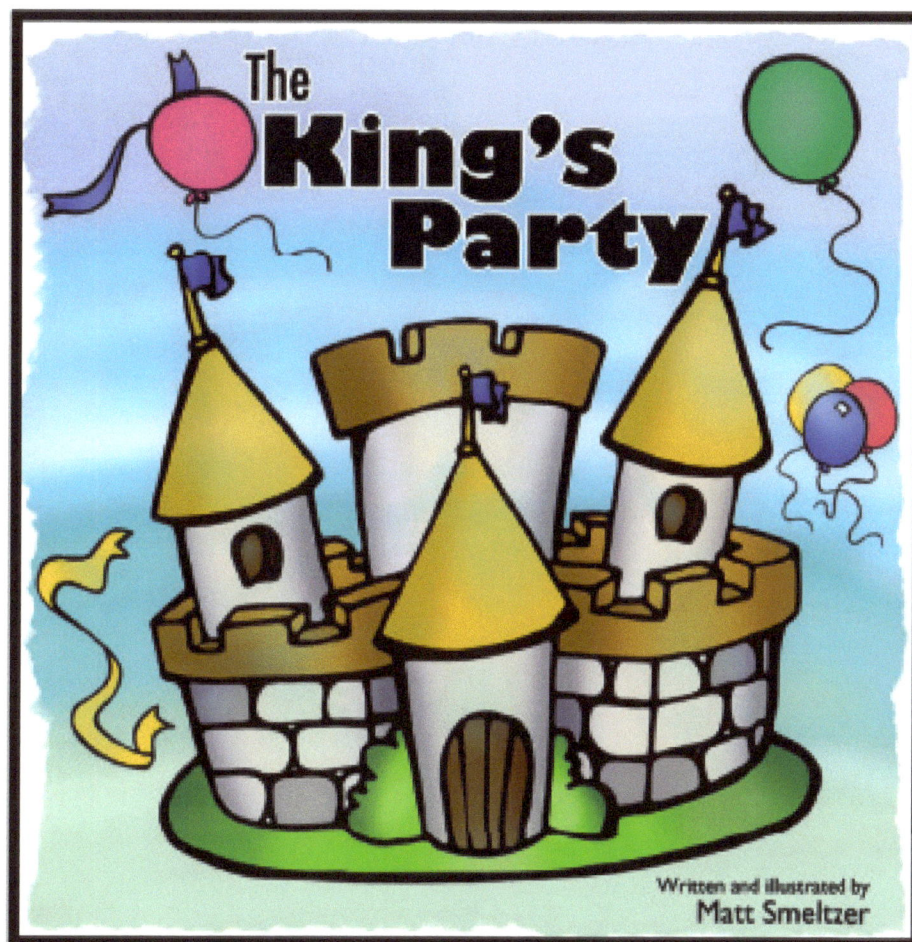

The King's Party

Written and illustrated by Matt Smeltzer

www.ingramcontent.com/pod-product-compliance
Lightning Source LLC
Chambersburg PA
CBHW042120040426
42449CB00002B/125